Snow Leopards

Snow Leopards

Patrick Merrick

THE CHILD'S WORLD®, INC.

Library of Congress Cataloging-in-Publication Data
Merrick, Patrick.
Snow leopards / by Patrick Merrick.
p.   cm.
Includes index.
Summary: Describes the physical characteristics, behavior,
habitat, and life cycle of snow leopards.
ISBN 1-56766-474-1 (lib. bdg. : alk. paper)
1. Snow leopard—Juvenile literature.
[1. Snow leopard. 2. Leopard.]   I. Title.
QL737.C23M47   1998
599.755'5—dc21   97-28748
CIP
AC

Photo Credits

© 1997 Bruce Montagne/Dembinsky Photo Assoc. Inc.: cover
© Comstock, Inc.: 30
© Daniel J. Cox/Natural Exposures: 20
© Darrell Gulin/Tony Stone Images: 13
© 1997 Fritz Pölking/Dembinsky Photo Assoc. Inc.: 15, 26
© James Martin/Tony Stone Images: 10
© 1996 Mark J. Thomas/Dembinsky Photo Assoc. Inc.: 9, 29
© Rosemary Calvert/Tony Stone Images: 19
© Russ Kinne/Comstock, Inc.: 16, 23
© Tim Davis/Tony Stone Images: 2, 6, 24

On the cover...

Front cover: This snow leopard is watching his surroundings.
Page 2: This snow leopard is lying in the snow.

Table of Contents

Meet the Snow Leopard!

High in the mountains of Asia, a fresh layer of snow has fallen. The air is clear and cold. A mountain goat walks by, searching for food among the rocks. While the mountain goat is looking for its food, something else is watching the mountain goat. The creature creeps closer. Suddenly, it pounces on the mountain goat and kills it. What type of creature is this? It's a snow leopard!

⇐ This adult snow leopard is playing in the snow.

What Are Snow Leopards?

Snow leopards belong to a group of animals called **mammals**. Mammals have hair all over their bodies. They also have warm blood and feed their babies milk from their bodies. Cows, dogs, bears, and people are mammals, too.

It is easy to see that snow leopards are very beautiful animals. ⇒

What Do Snow Leopards Look Like?

Like other leopards, snow leopards look like big cats. They are about five feet long and two feet tall. They have a wide nose, large eyes, and two small ears that stand straight up. To help it keep its balance, the snow leopard has a very long, thick tail, large paws, and short, strong legs.

Many people recognize snow leopards by their beautiful fur. The leopards' heads and bodies are covered with thick, whitish-gray fur with black spots.

Where Do Snow Leopards Live?

Many animals can live in only one type of place, or **environment**. If that environment is destroyed, the animals die. Snow leopards live only in the highest mountains of central Asia. There they roam in the small forests and cliffs on the mountainsides.

This snow leopard is resting on a snowy mountain. ⇒

Snow leopards are most active between sunset and early morning. They are mostly **nocturnal**, which means that they rest during the day and are active at night. While the leopard is resting, it stays in its **den**, a home hidden in the rocks.

This snow leopard has just come out of its den. ⇒

What Do Snow Leopards Eat?

Snow leopards are **predators**, or hunters. Predators hunt and eat other animals. A snow leopard's beautiful fur acts as **camouflage**, helping it blend in with its surroundings. Staying hidden, the leopard quietly watches other animals. When an animal comes very close, the leopard springs from its hiding spot and kills it. The snow leopard's favorite foods are wild sheep, wild pigs, deer, and other animals that live in the high mountains.

⇐ This snow leopard is hunting a small animal.

Do Snow Leopards Live Alone?

The snow leopard likes to live alone. The only time snow leopards stay together is during the mating season. Unlike other big cats, the snow leopard cannot roar. The only time a snow leopard makes a sound is when it is trying to attract a mate. The cry of a snow leopard sounds so strange, some people think it might be a snow monster coming down the mountain!

Snow leopards like this one have a strange cry. ⇒

How Are Baby Snow Leopards Born?

About 90 days after mating, the female snow leopard gives birth to about three babies. At first, the young leopards cannot even open their eyes. After about a week, the babies open their eyes and begin to move around. Soon they can go with their mother on hunting trips. The young snow leopards stay with their mother until they are about two years old. They learn how to hunt and find dens. When the young leopards are ready, they leave their mother and go off to live on their own.

⇐ This snow leopard cub is calling to its mother.

Do Snow Leopards Have Enemies?

Snow leopards do not have natural enemies. Only people can harm them. As more people move into the high mountains, they destroy the forests and cliffs where snow leopards hunt. Each day there is less food for snow leopards and fewer places for them to hide. As their environment is destroyed, the snow leopards are slowly dying out.

This snow leopard has been running in the snow. ⇒

Many people also kill snow leopards to make coats out of their beautiful fur. Some snow leopards are even killed for their bones. That is because some people believe the bones can cure illness. In fact, so many snow leopards have been killed, it is now against the law to hunt them.

Are Snow Leopards in Danger?

Snow leopards are **endangered**. This means that soon there may be no more snow leopards left in the entire world! Because it is so hard to reach the leopards' mountain home, scientists do not know how many are still living in the wild. There may be only about 3,000 wild snow leopards left.

⇐ These tracks belong to three wild snow leopards.

How Can We Save Snow Leopards?

Many countries are working to save these beautiful animals. China, Mongolia, and Nepal have parks in which the snow leopards can live safely. The country of Tibet is trying to save the leopards' mountain environment. And many zoos are trying to breed snow leopards to help increase their numbers.

This young snow leopard lives in a zoo in the United States. ⇒

Few animals are as graceful or as beautiful as the snow leopard. We are lucky to have the chance to see them. But we need to work hard to save their environment before these cats are gone forever. By caring for the snow leopards and their mountain home, we may be able to see these wonderful cats for a long time to come.

Glossary

camouflage (KAM–uh–flazh)
Camouflage is coloring that helps an animal blend in with its surroundings. Snow leopards use camouflage to hide from the animals they hunt.

endangered (en–DANE–jerd)
When a type of animal is endangered, it is in danger of dying out. Snow leopards are endangered because there are few left in the wild.

environment (en–VY–run–ment)
An animal's environment is the type of area in which it lives. The snow leopard's environment is the forests and cliffs of high Asian mountains.

den (DEN)
A den is a hollow spot in a tree or in the ground where an animal lives. Snow leopards live in dens in the mountains.

mammals (MA–mullz)
Mammals are animals that have hair and warm blood and feed their babies milk from their bodies. Snow leopards, cows, dogs, and people are all mammals.

nocturnal (nok–TUR–null)
Nocturnal animals sleep during the day and are active at night. Snow leopards are mostly nocturnal.

predator (PREH–duh–ter)
A predator is an animal that hunts other animals for food. Snow leopards are predators.

Index